WHAT'S MY LOGIN ?
PASSWORD TRACKER

Website : _____

USERNAME: _____
PASSWORD: _____
EMAIL LINKED: _____
NOTES: _____

Website : _____

USERNAME: _____
PASSWORD: _____
EMAIL LINKED: _____
NOTES: _____

Website : _____

USERNAME: _____
PASSWORD: _____
EMAIL LINKED: _____
NOTES: _____

Website : _____

USERNAME: _____
PASSWORD: _____
EMAIL LINKED: _____
NOTES: _____

WHAT'S MY LOGIN ?
PASSWORD TRACKER

Website :

USERNAME:

PASSWORD:

EMAIL LINKED:

NOTES:

Website :

USERNAME:

PASSWORD:

EMAIL LINKED:

NOTES:

Website :

USERNAME:

PASSWORD:

EMAIL LINKED:

NOTES:

Website :

USERNAME:

PASSWORD:

EMAIL LINKED:

NOTES:

WHAT'S MY LOGIN ?
PASSWORD TRACKER

Website :

USERNAME: _____
PASSWORD: _____
EMAIL LINKED: _____
NOTES: _____

Website :

USERNAME: _____
PASSWORD: _____
EMAIL LINKED: _____
NOTES: _____

Website :

USERNAME: _____
PASSWORD: _____
EMAIL LINKED: _____
NOTES: _____

Website :

USERNAME: _____
PASSWORD: _____
EMAIL LINKED: _____
NOTES: _____

WHAT'S MY LOGIN ?
PASSWORD TRACKER

Website :

USERNAME: _____
PASSWORD: _____
EMAIL LINKED: _____
NOTES: _____

Website :

USERNAME: _____
PASSWORD: _____
EMAIL LINKED: _____
NOTES: _____

Website :

USERNAME: _____
PASSWORD: _____
EMAIL LINKED: _____
NOTES: _____

Website :

USERNAME: _____
PASSWORD: _____
EMAIL LINKED: _____
NOTES: _____

WHAT'S MY LOGIN ?
PASSWORD TRACKER

Website : _____

USERNAME: _____
PASSWORD: _____
EMAIL LINKED: _____
NOTES: _____

Website : _____

USERNAME: _____
PASSWORD: _____
EMAIL LINKED: _____
NOTES: _____

Website : _____

USERNAME: _____
PASSWORD: _____
EMAIL LINKED: _____
NOTES: _____

Website : _____

USERNAME: _____
PASSWORD: _____
EMAIL LINKED: _____
NOTES: _____

WHAT'S MY LOGIN ?
PASSWORD TRACKER

Website : _____

USERNAME: _____

PASSWORD: _____

EMAIL LINKED: _____

NOTES: _____

Website : _____

USERNAME: _____

PASSWORD: _____

EMAIL LINKED: _____

NOTES: _____

Website : _____

USERNAME: _____

PASSWORD: _____

EMAIL LINKED: _____

NOTES: _____

Website : _____

USERNAME: _____

PASSWORD: _____

EMAIL LINKED: _____

NOTES: _____

WHAT'S MY LOGIN ?
PASSWORD TRACKER

Website :

USERNAME: _____

PASSWORD: _____

EMAIL LINKED: _____

NOTES: _____

Website :

USERNAME: _____

PASSWORD: _____

EMAIL LINKED: _____

NOTES: _____

Website :

USERNAME: _____

PASSWORD: _____

EMAIL LINKED: _____

NOTES: _____

Website :

USERNAME: _____

PASSWORD: _____

EMAIL LINKED: _____

NOTES: _____

WHAT'S MY LOGIN ?
PASSWORD TRACKER

Website :

USERNAME: _____
PASSWORD: _____
EMAIL LINKED: _____
NOTES: _____

Website :

USERNAME: _____
PASSWORD: _____
EMAIL LINKED: _____
NOTES: _____

Website :

USERNAME: _____
PASSWORD: _____
EMAIL LINKED: _____
NOTES: _____

Website :

USERNAME: _____
PASSWORD: _____
EMAIL LINKED: _____
NOTES: _____

WHAT'S MY LOGIN ?
PASSWORD TRACKER

Website : _____

USERNAME: _____
PASSWORD: _____
EMAIL LINKED: _____
NOTES: _____

Website : _____

USERNAME: _____
PASSWORD: _____
EMAIL LINKED: _____
NOTES: _____

Website : _____

USERNAME: _____
PASSWORD: _____
EMAIL LINKED: _____
NOTES: _____

Website : _____

USERNAME: _____
PASSWORD: _____
EMAIL LINKED: _____
NOTES: _____

WHAT'S MY LOGIN ?
PASSWORD TRACKER

Website :

USERNAME: _____
PASSWORD: _____
EMAIL LINKED: _____
NOTES: _____

Website :

USERNAME: _____
PASSWORD: _____
EMAIL LINKED: _____
NOTES: _____

Website :

USERNAME: _____
PASSWORD: _____
EMAIL LINKED: _____
NOTES: _____

Website :

USERNAME: _____
PASSWORD: _____
EMAIL LINKED: _____
NOTES: _____

WHAT'S MY LOGIN ?
PASSWORD TRACKER

Website :

USERNAME: _____
PASSWORD: _____
EMAIL LINKED: _____
NOTES: _____

Website :

USERNAME: _____
PASSWORD: _____
EMAIL LINKED: _____
NOTES: _____

Website :

USERNAME: _____
PASSWORD: _____
EMAIL LINKED: _____
NOTES: _____

Website :

USERNAME: _____
PASSWORD: _____
EMAIL LINKED: _____
NOTES: _____

WHAT'S MY LOGIN ?
PASSWORD TRACKER

Website :

USERNAME: _____
PASSWORD: _____
EMAIL LINKED: _____
NOTES: _____

Website :

USERNAME: _____
PASSWORD: _____
EMAIL LINKED: _____
NOTES: _____

Website :

USERNAME: _____
PASSWORD: _____
EMAIL LINKED: _____
NOTES: _____

Website :

USERNAME: _____
PASSWORD: _____
EMAIL LINKED: _____
NOTES: _____

WHAT'S MY LOGIN ?
PASSWORD TRACKER

Website : _____

USERNAME: _____
PASSWORD: _____
EMAIL LINKED: _____
NOTES: _____

Website : _____

USERNAME: _____
PASSWORD: _____
EMAIL LINKED: _____
NOTES: _____

Website : _____

USERNAME: _____
PASSWORD: _____
EMAIL LINKED: _____
NOTES: _____

Website : _____

USERNAME: _____
PASSWORD: _____
EMAIL LINKED: _____
NOTES: _____

WHAT'S MY LOGIN ?
PASSWORD TRACKER

Website :

USERNAME: _____
PASSWORD: _____
EMAIL LINKED: _____
NOTES: _____

Website :

USERNAME: _____
PASSWORD: _____
EMAIL LINKED: _____
NOTES: _____

Website :

USERNAME: _____
PASSWORD: _____
EMAIL LINKED: _____
NOTES: _____

Website :

USERNAME: _____
PASSWORD: _____
EMAIL LINKED: _____
NOTES: _____

WHAT'S MY LOGIN ?
PASSWORD TRACKER

Website : _____

USERNAME: _____
PASSWORD: _____
EMAIL LINKED: _____
NOTES: _____

Website : _____

USERNAME: _____
PASSWORD: _____
EMAIL LINKED: _____
NOTES: _____

Website : _____

USERNAME: _____
PASSWORD: _____
EMAIL LINKED: _____
NOTES: _____

Website : _____

USERNAME: _____
PASSWORD: _____
EMAIL LINKED: _____
NOTES: _____

WHAT'S MY LOGIN ?
PASSWORD TRACKER

Website :

USERNAME: _____

PASSWORD: _____

EMAIL LINKED: _____

NOTES: _____

Website :

USERNAME: _____

PASSWORD: _____

EMAIL LINKED: _____

NOTES: _____

Website :

USERNAME: _____

PASSWORD: _____

EMAIL LINKED: _____

NOTES: _____

Website :

USERNAME: _____

PASSWORD: _____

EMAIL LINKED: _____

NOTES: _____

WHAT'S MY LOGIN ?
PASSWORD TRACKER

Website : _____

USERNAME: _____
PASSWORD: _____
EMAIL LINKED: _____
NOTES: _____

Website : _____

USERNAME: _____
PASSWORD: _____
EMAIL LINKED: _____
NOTES: _____

Website : _____

USERNAME: _____
PASSWORD: _____
EMAIL LINKED: _____
NOTES: _____

Website : _____

USERNAME: _____
PASSWORD: _____
EMAIL LINKED: _____
NOTES: _____

WHAT'S MY LOGIN ?
PASSWORD TRACKER

Website :

USERNAME: _____
PASSWORD: _____
EMAIL LINKED: _____
NOTES: _____

Website :

USERNAME: _____
PASSWORD: _____
EMAIL LINKED: _____
NOTES: _____

Website :

USERNAME: _____
PASSWORD: _____
EMAIL LINKED: _____
NOTES: _____

Website :

USERNAME: _____
PASSWORD: _____
EMAIL LINKED: _____
NOTES: _____

WHAT'S MY LOGIN ?
PASSWORD TRACKER

Website :

USERNAME: _____
PASSWORD: _____
EMAIL LINKED: _____
NOTES: _____

Website :

USERNAME: _____
PASSWORD: _____
EMAIL LINKED: _____
NOTES: _____

Website :

USERNAME: _____
PASSWORD: _____
EMAIL LINKED: _____
NOTES: _____

Website :

USERNAME: _____
PASSWORD: _____
EMAIL LINKED: _____
NOTES: _____

WHAT'S MY LOGIN ?
PASSWORD TRACKER

Website :

USERNAME: _____
PASSWORD: _____
EMAIL LINKED: _____
NOTES: _____

Website :

USERNAME: _____
PASSWORD: _____
EMAIL LINKED: _____
NOTES: _____

Website :

USERNAME: _____
PASSWORD: _____
EMAIL LINKED: _____
NOTES: _____

Website :

USERNAME: _____
PASSWORD: _____
EMAIL LINKED: _____
NOTES: _____

WHAT'S MY LOGIN ?
PASSWORD TRACKER

Website :

USERNAME: _____
PASSWORD: _____
EMAIL LINKED: _____
NOTES: _____

Website :

USERNAME: _____
PASSWORD: _____
EMAIL LINKED: _____
NOTES: _____

Website :

USERNAME: _____
PASSWORD: _____
EMAIL LINKED: _____
NOTES: _____

Website :

USERNAME: _____
PASSWORD: _____
EMAIL LINKED: _____
NOTES: _____

WHAT'S MY LOGIN ?
PASSWORD TRACKER

Website :

USERNAME:
PASSWORD:
EMAIL LINKED:
NOTES:

Website :

USERNAME:
PASSWORD:
EMAIL LINKED:
NOTES:

Website :

USERNAME:
PASSWORD:
EMAIL LINKED:
NOTES:

Website :

USERNAME:
PASSWORD:
EMAIL LINKED:
NOTES:

WHAT'S MY LOGIN ?
PASSWORD TRACKER

Website :

USERNAME: _____
PASSWORD: _____
EMAIL LINKED: _____
NOTES: _____

Website :

USERNAME: _____
PASSWORD: _____
EMAIL LINKED: _____
NOTES: _____

Website :

USERNAME: _____
PASSWORD: _____
EMAIL LINKED: _____
NOTES: _____

Website :

USERNAME: _____
PASSWORD: _____
EMAIL LINKED: _____
NOTES: _____

WHAT'S MY LOGIN ?
PASSWORD TRACKER

Website : _____

USERNAME: _____
PASSWORD: _____
EMAIL LINKED: _____
NOTES: _____

Website : _____

USERNAME: _____
PASSWORD: _____
EMAIL LINKED: _____
NOTES: _____

Website : _____

USERNAME: _____
PASSWORD: _____
EMAIL LINKED: _____
NOTES: _____

Website : _____

USERNAME: _____
PASSWORD: _____
EMAIL LINKED: _____
NOTES: _____

WHAT'S MY LOGIN ?
PASSWORD TRACKER

Website : _____

USERNAME: _____
PASSWORD: _____
EMAIL LINKED: _____
NOTES: _____

Website : _____

USERNAME: _____
PASSWORD: _____
EMAIL LINKED: _____
NOTES: _____

Website : _____

USERNAME: _____
PASSWORD: _____
EMAIL LINKED: _____
NOTES: _____

Website : _____

USERNAME: _____
PASSWORD: _____
EMAIL LINKED: _____
NOTES: _____

WHAT'S MY LOGIN ?
PASSWORD TRACKER

Website :

USERNAME: _____
PASSWORD: _____
EMAIL LINKED: _____
NOTES: _____

Website :

USERNAME: _____
PASSWORD: _____
EMAIL LINKED: _____
NOTES: _____

Website :

USERNAME: _____
PASSWORD: _____
EMAIL LINKED: _____
NOTES: _____

Website :

USERNAME: _____
PASSWORD: _____
EMAIL LINKED: _____
NOTES: _____

WHAT'S MY LOGIN ?
PASSWORD TRACKER

Website :

USERNAME: _____
PASSWORD: _____
EMAIL LINKED: _____
NOTES: _____

Website :

USERNAME: _____
PASSWORD: _____
EMAIL LINKED: _____
NOTES: _____

Website :

USERNAME: _____
PASSWORD: _____
EMAIL LINKED: _____
NOTES: _____

Website :

USERNAME: _____
PASSWORD: _____
EMAIL LINKED: _____
NOTES: _____

WHAT'S MY LOGIN ?
PASSWORD TRACKER

Website :

USERNAME: _____
PASSWORD: _____
EMAIL LINKED: _____
NOTES: _____

Website :

USERNAME: _____
PASSWORD: _____
EMAIL LINKED: _____
NOTES: _____

Website :

USERNAME: _____
PASSWORD: _____
EMAIL LINKED: _____
NOTES: _____

Website :

USERNAME: _____
PASSWORD: _____
EMAIL LINKED: _____
NOTES: _____

WHAT'S MY LOGIN ?
PASSWORD TRACKER

Website :

USERNAME: _____

PASSWORD: _____

EMAIL LINKED: _____

NOTES: _____

Website :

USERNAME: _____

PASSWORD: _____

EMAIL LINKED: _____

NOTES: _____

Website :

USERNAME: _____

PASSWORD: _____

EMAIL LINKED: _____

NOTES: _____

Website :

USERNAME: _____

PASSWORD: _____

EMAIL LINKED: _____

NOTES: _____

WHAT'S MY LOGIN ?
PASSWORD TRACKER

Website :

USERNAME: _____
PASSWORD: _____
EMAIL LINKED: _____
NOTES: _____

Website :

USERNAME: _____
PASSWORD: _____
EMAIL LINKED: _____
NOTES: _____

Website :

USERNAME: _____
PASSWORD: _____
EMAIL LINKED: _____
NOTES: _____

Website :

USERNAME: _____
PASSWORD: _____
EMAIL LINKED: _____
NOTES: _____

WHAT'S MY LOGIN ?
PASSWORD TRACKER

Website :

USERNAME: _____
PASSWORD: _____
EMAIL LINKED: _____
NOTES: _____

Website :

USERNAME: _____
PASSWORD: _____
EMAIL LINKED: _____
NOTES: _____

Website :

USERNAME: _____
PASSWORD: _____
EMAIL LINKED: _____
NOTES: _____

Website :

USERNAME: _____
PASSWORD: _____
EMAIL LINKED: _____
NOTES: _____

WHAT'S MY LOGIN ?
PASSWORD TRACKER

Website :

USERNAME: _____
PASSWORD: _____
EMAIL LINKED: _____
NOTES: _____

Website :

USERNAME: _____
PASSWORD: _____
EMAIL LINKED: _____
NOTES: _____

Website :

USERNAME: _____
PASSWORD: _____
EMAIL LINKED: _____
NOTES: _____

Website :

USERNAME: _____
PASSWORD: _____
EMAIL LINKED: _____
NOTES: _____

WHAT'S MY LOGIN ?
PASSWORD TRACKER

Website :

USERNAME: _____

PASSWORD: _____

EMAIL LINKED: _____

NOTES: _____

Website :

USERNAME: _____

PASSWORD: _____

EMAIL LINKED: _____

NOTES: _____

Website :

USERNAME: _____

PASSWORD: _____

EMAIL LINKED: _____

NOTES: _____

Website :

USERNAME: _____

PASSWORD: _____

EMAIL LINKED: _____

NOTES: _____

WHAT'S MY LOGIN ?
PASSWORD TRACKER

Website :

USERNAME: _____
PASSWORD: _____
EMAIL LINKED: _____
NOTES: _____

Website :

USERNAME: _____
PASSWORD: _____
EMAIL LINKED: _____
NOTES: _____

Website :

USERNAME: _____
PASSWORD: _____
EMAIL LINKED: _____
NOTES: _____

Website :

USERNAME: _____
PASSWORD: _____
EMAIL LINKED: _____
NOTES: _____

WHAT'S MY LOGIN ?
PASSWORD TRACKER

Website :

USERNAME: _____

PASSWORD: _____

EMAIL LINKED: _____

NOTES: _____

Website :

USERNAME: _____

PASSWORD: _____

EMAIL LINKED: _____

NOTES: _____

Website :

USERNAME: _____

PASSWORD: _____

EMAIL LINKED: _____

NOTES: _____

Website :

USERNAME: _____

PASSWORD: _____

EMAIL LINKED: _____

NOTES: _____

WHAT'S MY LOGIN ?
PASSWORD TRACKER

Website :

USERNAME: _____
PASSWORD: _____
EMAIL LINKED: _____
NOTES: _____

Website :

USERNAME: _____
PASSWORD: _____
EMAIL LINKED: _____
NOTES: _____

Website :

USERNAME: _____
PASSWORD: _____
EMAIL LINKED: _____
NOTES: _____

Website :

USERNAME: _____
PASSWORD: _____
EMAIL LINKED: _____
NOTES: _____

WHAT'S MY LOGIN ?
PASSWORD TRACKER

Website : _____

USERNAME: _____
PASSWORD: _____
EMAIL LINKED: _____
NOTES: _____

Website : _____

USERNAME: _____
PASSWORD: _____
EMAIL LINKED: _____
NOTES: _____

Website : _____

USERNAME: _____
PASSWORD: _____
EMAIL LINKED: _____
NOTES: _____

Website : _____

USERNAME: _____
PASSWORD: _____
EMAIL LINKED: _____
NOTES: _____

WHAT'S MY LOGIN ?
PASSWORD TRACKER

Website : _____

USERNAME: _____
PASSWORD: _____
EMAIL LINKED: _____
NOTES: _____

Website : _____

USERNAME: _____
PASSWORD: _____
EMAIL LINKED: _____
NOTES: _____

Website : _____

USERNAME: _____
PASSWORD: _____
EMAIL LINKED: _____
NOTES: _____

Website : _____

USERNAME: _____
PASSWORD: _____
EMAIL LINKED: _____
NOTES: _____

WHAT'S MY LOGIN ?
PASSWORD TRACKER

Website :

USERNAME: _____
PASSWORD: _____
EMAIL LINKED: _____
NOTES: _____

Website :

USERNAME: _____
PASSWORD: _____
EMAIL LINKED: _____
NOTES: _____

Website :

USERNAME: _____
PASSWORD: _____
EMAIL LINKED: _____
NOTES: _____

Website :

USERNAME: _____
PASSWORD: _____
EMAIL LINKED: _____
NOTES: _____

WHAT'S MY LOGIN ?
PASSWORD TRACKER

Website :

USERNAME: _____

PASSWORD: _____

EMAIL LINKED: _____

NOTES: _____

Website :

USERNAME: _____

PASSWORD: _____

EMAIL LINKED: _____

NOTES: _____

Website :

USERNAME: _____

PASSWORD: _____

EMAIL LINKED: _____

NOTES: _____

Website :

USERNAME: _____

PASSWORD: _____

EMAIL LINKED: _____

NOTES: _____

WHAT'S MY LOGIN ?
PASSWORD TRACKER

Website :

USERNAME: _____
PASSWORD: _____
EMAIL LINKED: _____
NOTES: _____

Website :

USERNAME: _____
PASSWORD: _____
EMAIL LINKED: _____
NOTES: _____

Website :

USERNAME: _____
PASSWORD: _____
EMAIL LINKED: _____
NOTES: _____

Website :

USERNAME: _____
PASSWORD: _____
EMAIL LINKED: _____
NOTES: _____

WHAT'S MY LOGIN ?
PASSWORD TRACKER

Website :

USERNAME: _____
PASSWORD: _____
EMAIL LINKED: _____
NOTES: _____

Website :

USERNAME: _____
PASSWORD: _____
EMAIL LINKED: _____
NOTES: _____

Website :

USERNAME: _____
PASSWORD: _____
EMAIL LINKED: _____
NOTES: _____

Website :

USERNAME: _____
PASSWORD: _____
EMAIL LINKED: _____
NOTES: _____

WHAT'S MY LOGIN ?
PASSWORD TRACKER

Website :

USERNAME: _____

PASSWORD: _____

EMAIL LINKED: _____

NOTES: _____

Website :

USERNAME: _____

PASSWORD: _____

EMAIL LINKED: _____

NOTES: _____

Website :

USERNAME: _____

PASSWORD: _____

EMAIL LINKED: _____

NOTES: _____

Website :

USERNAME: _____

PASSWORD: _____

EMAIL LINKED: _____

NOTES: _____

WHAT'S MY LOGIN ?
PASSWORD TRACKER

Website :

USERNAME: _____
PASSWORD: _____
EMAIL LINKED: _____
NOTES: _____

Website :

USERNAME: _____
PASSWORD: _____
EMAIL LINKED: _____
NOTES: _____

Website :

USERNAME: _____
PASSWORD: _____
EMAIL LINKED: _____
NOTES: _____

Website :

USERNAME: _____
PASSWORD: _____
EMAIL LINKED: _____
NOTES: _____

WHAT'S MY LOGIN ?
PASSWORD TRACKER

Website :

USERNAME: _____
PASSWORD: _____
EMAIL LINKED: _____
NOTES: _____

Website :

USERNAME: _____
PASSWORD: _____
EMAIL LINKED: _____
NOTES: _____

Website :

USERNAME: _____
PASSWORD: _____
EMAIL LINKED: _____
NOTES: _____

Website :

USERNAME: _____
PASSWORD: _____
EMAIL LINKED: _____
NOTES: _____

WHAT'S MY LOGIN ?
PASSWORD TRACKER

Website :

USERNAME: _____
PASSWORD: _____
EMAIL LINKED: _____
NOTES: _____

Website :

USERNAME: _____
PASSWORD: _____
EMAIL LINKED: _____
NOTES: _____

Website :

USERNAME: _____
PASSWORD: _____
EMAIL LINKED: _____
NOTES: _____

Website :

USERNAME: _____
PASSWORD: _____
EMAIL LINKED: _____
NOTES: _____

WHAT'S MY LOGIN ?
PASSWORD TRACKER

Website :

USERNAME: _____
PASSWORD: _____
EMAIL LINKED: _____
NOTES: _____

Website :

USERNAME: _____
PASSWORD: _____
EMAIL LINKED: _____
NOTES: _____

Website :

USERNAME: _____
PASSWORD: _____
EMAIL LINKED: _____
NOTES: _____

Website :

USERNAME: _____
PASSWORD: _____
EMAIL LINKED: _____
NOTES: _____

WHAT'S MY LOGIN ?
PASSWORD TRACKER

Website :

USERNAME: _____
PASSWORD: _____
EMAIL LINKED: _____
NOTES: _____

Website :

USERNAME: _____
PASSWORD: _____
EMAIL LINKED: _____
NOTES: _____

Website :

USERNAME: _____
PASSWORD: _____
EMAIL LINKED: _____
NOTES: _____

Website :

USERNAME: _____
PASSWORD: _____
EMAIL LINKED: _____
NOTES: _____

WHAT'S MY LOGIN ?
PASSWORD TRACKER

Website : _____

USERNAME: _____
PASSWORD: _____
EMAIL LINKED: _____
NOTES: _____

Website : _____

USERNAME: _____
PASSWORD: _____
EMAIL LINKED: _____
NOTES: _____

Website : _____

USERNAME: _____
PASSWORD: _____
EMAIL LINKED: _____
NOTES: _____

Website : _____

USERNAME: _____
PASSWORD: _____
EMAIL LINKED: _____
NOTES: _____

WHAT'S MY LOGIN ?
PASSWORD TRACKER

Website : _____

USERNAME: _____
PASSWORD: _____
EMAIL LINKED: _____
NOTES: _____

Website : _____

USERNAME: _____
PASSWORD: _____
EMAIL LINKED: _____
NOTES: _____

Website : _____

USERNAME: _____
PASSWORD: _____
EMAIL LINKED: _____
NOTES: _____

Website : _____

USERNAME: _____
PASSWORD: _____
EMAIL LINKED: _____
NOTES: _____

WHAT'S MY LOGIN ?
PASSWORD TRACKER

Website :

USERNAME: _____

PASSWORD: _____

EMAIL LINKED: _____

NOTES: _____

Website :

USERNAME: _____

PASSWORD: _____

EMAIL LINKED: _____

NOTES: _____

Website :

USERNAME: _____

PASSWORD: _____

EMAIL LINKED: _____

NOTES: _____

Website :

USERNAME: _____

PASSWORD: _____

EMAIL LINKED: _____

NOTES: _____

WHAT'S MY LOGIN ?
PASSWORD TRACKER

Website :

USERNAME: _____
PASSWORD: _____
EMAIL LINKED: _____
NOTES: _____

Website :

USERNAME: _____
PASSWORD: _____
EMAIL LINKED: _____
NOTES: _____

Website :

USERNAME: _____
PASSWORD: _____
EMAIL LINKED: _____
NOTES: _____

Website :

USERNAME: _____
PASSWORD: _____
EMAIL LINKED: _____
NOTES: _____

WHAT'S MY LOGIN ?
PASSWORD TRACKER

Website :

USERNAME: _____
PASSWORD: _____
EMAIL LINKED: _____
NOTES: _____

Website :

USERNAME: _____
PASSWORD: _____
EMAIL LINKED: _____
NOTES: _____

Website :

USERNAME: _____
PASSWORD: _____
EMAIL LINKED: _____
NOTES: _____

Website :

USERNAME: _____
PASSWORD: _____
EMAIL LINKED: _____
NOTES: _____

WHAT'S MY LOGIN ?
PASSWORD TRACKER

Website :

USERNAME: _____
PASSWORD: _____
EMAIL LINKED: _____
NOTES: _____

Website :

USERNAME: _____
PASSWORD: _____
EMAIL LINKED: _____
NOTES: _____

Website :

USERNAME: _____
PASSWORD: _____
EMAIL LINKED: _____
NOTES: _____

Website :

USERNAME: _____
PASSWORD: _____
EMAIL LINKED: _____
NOTES: _____

WHAT'S MY LOGIN ?
PASSWORD TRACKER

Website :

USERNAME: _____
PASSWORD: _____
EMAIL LINKED: _____
NOTES: _____

Website :

USERNAME: _____
PASSWORD: _____
EMAIL LINKED: _____
NOTES: _____

Website :

USERNAME: _____
PASSWORD: _____
EMAIL LINKED: _____
NOTES: _____

Website :

USERNAME: _____
PASSWORD: _____
EMAIL LINKED: _____
NOTES: _____

WHAT'S MY LOGIN ?
PASSWORD TRACKER

Website :

USERNAME: _____
PASSWORD: _____
EMAIL LINKED: _____
NOTES: _____

Website :

USERNAME: _____
PASSWORD: _____
EMAIL LINKED: _____
NOTES: _____

Website :

USERNAME: _____
PASSWORD: _____
EMAIL LINKED: _____
NOTES: _____

Website :

USERNAME: _____
PASSWORD: _____
EMAIL LINKED: _____
NOTES: _____

WHAT'S MY LOGIN ?
PASSWORD TRACKER

Website : _____

USERNAME: _____
PASSWORD: _____
EMAIL LINKED: _____
NOTES: _____

Website : _____

USERNAME: _____
PASSWORD: _____
EMAIL LINKED: _____
NOTES: _____

Website : _____

USERNAME: _____
PASSWORD: _____
EMAIL LINKED: _____
NOTES: _____

Website : _____

USERNAME: _____
PASSWORD: _____
EMAIL LINKED: _____
NOTES: _____

WHAT'S MY LOGIN ?
PASSWORD TRACKER

Website :

USERNAME: _____
PASSWORD: _____
EMAIL LINKED: _____
NOTES: _____

Website :

USERNAME: _____
PASSWORD: _____
EMAIL LINKED: _____
NOTES: _____

Website :

USERNAME: _____
PASSWORD: _____
EMAIL LINKED: _____
NOTES: _____

Website :

USERNAME: _____
PASSWORD: _____
EMAIL LINKED: _____
NOTES: _____

WHAT'S MY LOGIN ?
PASSWORD TRACKER

Website :

USERNAME: _____
PASSWORD: _____
EMAIL LINKED: _____
NOTES: _____

Website :

USERNAME: _____
PASSWORD: _____
EMAIL LINKED: _____
NOTES: _____

Website :

USERNAME: _____
PASSWORD: _____
EMAIL LINKED: _____
NOTES: _____

Website :

USERNAME: _____
PASSWORD: _____
EMAIL LINKED: _____
NOTES: _____

WHAT'S MY LOGIN ?
PASSWORD TRACKER

Website :

USERNAME: _____
PASSWORD: _____
EMAIL LINKED: _____
NOTES: _____

Website :

USERNAME: _____
PASSWORD: _____
EMAIL LINKED: _____
NOTES: _____

Website :

USERNAME: _____
PASSWORD: _____
EMAIL LINKED: _____
NOTES: _____

Website :

USERNAME: _____
PASSWORD: _____
EMAIL LINKED: _____
NOTES: _____

WHAT'S MY LOGIN ?
PASSWORD TRACKER

Website :

USERNAME: _____
PASSWORD: _____
EMAIL LINKED: _____
NOTES: _____

Website :

USERNAME: _____
PASSWORD: _____
EMAIL LINKED: _____
NOTES: _____

Website :

USERNAME: _____
PASSWORD: _____
EMAIL LINKED: _____
NOTES: _____

Website :

USERNAME: _____
PASSWORD: _____
EMAIL LINKED: _____
NOTES: _____

WHAT'S MY LOGIN ?
PASSWORD TRACKER

Website :

USERNAME: _____
PASSWORD: _____
EMAIL LINKED: _____
NOTES: _____

Website :

USERNAME: _____
PASSWORD: _____
EMAIL LINKED: _____
NOTES: _____

Website :

USERNAME: _____
PASSWORD: _____
EMAIL LINKED: _____
NOTES: _____

Website :

USERNAME: _____
PASSWORD: _____
EMAIL LINKED: _____
NOTES: _____

WHAT'S MY LOGIN ?
PASSWORD TRACKER

Website :

USERNAME: _____
PASSWORD: _____
EMAIL LINKED: _____
NOTES: _____

Website :

USERNAME: _____
PASSWORD: _____
EMAIL LINKED: _____
NOTES: _____

Website :

USERNAME: _____
PASSWORD: _____
EMAIL LINKED: _____
NOTES: _____

Website :

USERNAME: _____
PASSWORD: _____
EMAIL LINKED: _____
NOTES: _____

WHAT'S MY LOGIN ?
PASSWORD TRACKER

Website :

USERNAME: _____
PASSWORD: _____
EMAIL LINKED: _____
NOTES: _____

Website :

USERNAME: _____
PASSWORD: _____
EMAIL LINKED: _____
NOTES: _____

Website :

USERNAME: _____
PASSWORD: _____
EMAIL LINKED: _____
NOTES: _____

Website :

USERNAME: _____
PASSWORD: _____
EMAIL LINKED: _____
NOTES: _____

WHAT'S MY LOGIN ?
PASSWORD TRACKER

Website :

USERNAME: _____
PASSWORD: _____
EMAIL LINKED: _____
NOTES: _____

Website :

USERNAME: _____
PASSWORD: _____
EMAIL LINKED: _____
NOTES: _____

Website :

USERNAME: _____
PASSWORD: _____
EMAIL LINKED: _____
NOTES: _____

Website :

USERNAME: _____
PASSWORD: _____
EMAIL LINKED: _____
NOTES: _____

WHAT'S MY LOGIN ?
PASSWORD TRACKER

Website :

USERNAME:
PASSWORD:
EMAIL LINKED:
NOTES:

Website :

USERNAME:
PASSWORD:
EMAIL LINKED:
NOTES:

Website :

USERNAME:
PASSWORD:
EMAIL LINKED:
NOTES:

Website :

USERNAME:
PASSWORD:
EMAIL LINKED:
NOTES:

WHAT'S MY LOGIN ?
PASSWORD TRACKER

Website :

USERNAME: _____

PASSWORD: _____

EMAIL LINKED: _____

NOTES: _____

Website :

USERNAME: _____

PASSWORD: _____

EMAIL LINKED: _____

NOTES: _____

Website :

USERNAME: _____

PASSWORD: _____

EMAIL LINKED: _____

NOTES: _____

Website :

USERNAME: _____

PASSWORD: _____

EMAIL LINKED: _____

NOTES: _____

WHAT'S MY LOGIN ?
PASSWORD TRACKER

Website :

USERNAME: _____
PASSWORD: _____
EMAIL LINKED: _____
NOTES: _____

Website :

USERNAME: _____
PASSWORD: _____
EMAIL LINKED: _____
NOTES: _____

Website :

USERNAME: _____
PASSWORD: _____
EMAIL LINKED: _____
NOTES: _____

Website :

USERNAME: _____
PASSWORD: _____
EMAIL LINKED: _____
NOTES: _____

WHAT'S MY LOGIN ?
PASSWORD TRACKER

Website :

USERNAME: _____
PASSWORD: _____
EMAIL LINKED: _____
NOTES: _____

Website :

USERNAME: _____
PASSWORD: _____
EMAIL LINKED: _____
NOTES: _____

Website :

USERNAME: _____
PASSWORD: _____
EMAIL LINKED: _____
NOTES: _____

Website :

USERNAME: _____
PASSWORD: _____
EMAIL LINKED: _____
NOTES: _____

WHAT'S MY LOGIN ?
PASSWORD TRACKER

Website :

USERNAME: _____
PASSWORD: _____
EMAIL LINKED: _____
NOTES: _____

Website :

USERNAME: _____
PASSWORD: _____
EMAIL LINKED: _____
NOTES: _____

Website :

USERNAME: _____
PASSWORD: _____
EMAIL LINKED: _____
NOTES: _____

Website :

USERNAME: _____
PASSWORD: _____
EMAIL LINKED: _____
NOTES: _____

WHAT'S MY LOGIN ?
PASSWORD TRACKER

Website :

USERNAME: _____
PASSWORD: _____
EMAIL LINKED: _____
NOTES: _____

Website :

USERNAME: _____
PASSWORD: _____
EMAIL LINKED: _____
NOTES: _____

Website :

USERNAME: _____
PASSWORD: _____
EMAIL LINKED: _____
NOTES: _____

Website :

USERNAME: _____
PASSWORD: _____
EMAIL LINKED: _____
NOTES: _____

WHAT'S MY LOGIN ?
PASSWORD TRACKER

Website :

USERNAME: _____
PASSWORD: _____
EMAIL LINKED: _____
NOTES: _____

Website :

USERNAME: _____
PASSWORD: _____
EMAIL LINKED: _____
NOTES: _____

Website :

USERNAME: _____
PASSWORD: _____
EMAIL LINKED: _____
NOTES: _____

Website :

USERNAME: _____
PASSWORD: _____
EMAIL LINKED: _____
NOTES: _____

WHAT'S MY LOGIN ?
PASSWORD TRACKER

Website : _____

USERNAME: _____
PASSWORD: _____
EMAIL LINKED: _____
NOTES: _____

Website : _____

USERNAME: _____
PASSWORD: _____
EMAIL LINKED: _____
NOTES: _____

Website : _____

USERNAME: _____
PASSWORD: _____
EMAIL LINKED: _____
NOTES: _____

Website : _____

USERNAME: _____
PASSWORD: _____
EMAIL LINKED: _____
NOTES: _____

WHAT'S MY LOGIN ?
PASSWORD TRACKER

Website :

USERNAME: _____
PASSWORD: _____
EMAIL LINKED: _____
NOTES: _____

Website :

USERNAME: _____
PASSWORD: _____
EMAIL LINKED: _____
NOTES: _____

Website :

USERNAME: _____
PASSWORD: _____
EMAIL LINKED: _____
NOTES: _____

Website :

USERNAME: _____
PASSWORD: _____
EMAIL LINKED: _____
NOTES: _____

WHAT'S MY LOGIN ?
PASSWORD TRACKER

Website :

USERNAME: _____

PASSWORD: _____

EMAIL LINKED: _____

NOTES: _____

Website :

USERNAME: _____

PASSWORD: _____

EMAIL LINKED: _____

NOTES: _____

Website :

USERNAME: _____

PASSWORD: _____

EMAIL LINKED: _____

NOTES: _____

Website :

USERNAME: _____

PASSWORD: _____

EMAIL LINKED: _____

NOTES: _____

WHAT'S MY LOGIN ?
PASSWORD TRACKER

Website :

USERNAME: _____
PASSWORD: _____
EMAIL LINKED: _____
NOTES: _____

Website :

USERNAME: _____
PASSWORD: _____
EMAIL LINKED: _____
NOTES: _____

Website :

USERNAME: _____
PASSWORD: _____
EMAIL LINKED: _____
NOTES: _____

Website :

USERNAME: _____
PASSWORD: _____
EMAIL LINKED: _____
NOTES: _____

WHAT'S MY LOGIN ?
PASSWORD TRACKER

Website : _____

USERNAME: _____
PASSWORD: _____
EMAIL LINKED: _____
NOTES: _____

Website : _____

USERNAME: _____
PASSWORD: _____
EMAIL LINKED: _____
NOTES: _____

Website : _____

USERNAME: _____
PASSWORD: _____
EMAIL LINKED: _____
NOTES: _____

Website : _____

USERNAME: _____
PASSWORD: _____
EMAIL LINKED: _____
NOTES: _____

WHAT'S MY LOGIN ?
PASSWORD TRACKER

Website :

USERNAME: _____
PASSWORD: _____
EMAIL LINKED: _____
NOTES: _____

Website :

USERNAME: _____
PASSWORD: _____
EMAIL LINKED: _____
NOTES: _____

Website :

USERNAME: _____
PASSWORD: _____
EMAIL LINKED: _____
NOTES: _____

Website :

USERNAME: _____
PASSWORD: _____
EMAIL LINKED: _____
NOTES: _____

WHAT'S MY LOGIN ?
PASSWORD TRACKER

Website :

USERNAME: _____
PASSWORD: _____
EMAIL LINKED: _____
NOTES: _____

Website :

USERNAME: _____
PASSWORD: _____
EMAIL LINKED: _____
NOTES: _____

Website :

USERNAME: _____
PASSWORD: _____
EMAIL LINKED: _____
NOTES: _____

Website :

USERNAME: _____
PASSWORD: _____
EMAIL LINKED: _____
NOTES: _____

WHAT'S MY LOGIN ?
PASSWORD TRACKER

Website :

USERNAME: _____

PASSWORD: _____

EMAIL LINKED: _____

NOTES: _____

Website :

USERNAME: _____

PASSWORD: _____

EMAIL LINKED: _____

NOTES: _____

Website :

USERNAME: _____

PASSWORD: _____

EMAIL LINKED: _____

NOTES: _____

Website :

USERNAME: _____

PASSWORD: _____

EMAIL LINKED: _____

NOTES: _____

WHAT'S MY LOGIN ?
PASSWORD TRACKER

Website :

USERNAME: _____
PASSWORD: _____
EMAIL LINKED: _____
NOTES: _____

Website :

USERNAME: _____
PASSWORD: _____
EMAIL LINKED: _____
NOTES: _____

Website :

USERNAME: _____
PASSWORD: _____
EMAIL LINKED: _____
NOTES: _____

Website :

USERNAME: _____
PASSWORD: _____
EMAIL LINKED: _____
NOTES: _____

WHAT'S MY LOGIN ?
PASSWORD TRACKER

Website :

USERNAME: _____
PASSWORD: _____
EMAIL LINKED: _____
NOTES: _____

Website :

USERNAME: _____
PASSWORD: _____
EMAIL LINKED: _____
NOTES: _____

Website :

USERNAME: _____
PASSWORD: _____
EMAIL LINKED: _____
NOTES: _____

Website :

USERNAME: _____
PASSWORD: _____
EMAIL LINKED: _____
NOTES: _____

WHAT'S MY LOGIN ?
PASSWORD TRACKER

Website :

USERNAME: _____
PASSWORD: _____
EMAIL LINKED: _____
NOTES: _____

Website :

USERNAME: _____
PASSWORD: _____
EMAIL LINKED: _____
NOTES: _____

Website :

USERNAME: _____
PASSWORD: _____
EMAIL LINKED: _____
NOTES: _____

Website :

USERNAME: _____
PASSWORD: _____
EMAIL LINKED: _____
NOTES: _____

WHAT'S MY LOGIN ?
PASSWORD TRACKER

Website :

USERNAME: _____

PASSWORD: _____

EMAIL LINKED: _____

NOTES: _____

Website :

USERNAME: _____

PASSWORD: _____

EMAIL LINKED: _____

NOTES: _____

Website :

USERNAME: _____

PASSWORD: _____

EMAIL LINKED: _____

NOTES: _____

Website :

USERNAME: _____

PASSWORD: _____

EMAIL LINKED: _____

NOTES: _____

WHAT'S MY LOGIN ?
PASSWORD TRACKER

Website :

USERNAME: _____
PASSWORD: _____
EMAIL LINKED: _____
NOTES: _____

Website :

USERNAME: _____
PASSWORD: _____
EMAIL LINKED: _____
NOTES: _____

Website :

USERNAME: _____
PASSWORD: _____
EMAIL LINKED: _____
NOTES: _____

Website :

USERNAME: _____
PASSWORD: _____
EMAIL LINKED: _____
NOTES: _____

WHAT'S MY LOGIN ?
PASSWORD TRACKER

Website :

USERNAME: _____
PASSWORD: _____
EMAIL LINKED: _____
NOTES: _____

Website :

USERNAME: _____
PASSWORD: _____
EMAIL LINKED: _____
NOTES: _____

Website :

USERNAME: _____
PASSWORD: _____
EMAIL LINKED: _____
NOTES: _____

Website :

USERNAME: _____
PASSWORD: _____
EMAIL LINKED: _____
NOTES: _____

WHAT'S MY LOGIN ?
PASSWORD TRACKER

Website :

USERNAME: _____
PASSWORD: _____
EMAIL LINKED: _____
NOTES: _____

Website :

USERNAME: _____
PASSWORD: _____
EMAIL LINKED: _____
NOTES: _____

Website :

USERNAME: _____
PASSWORD: _____
EMAIL LINKED: _____
NOTES: _____

Website :

USERNAME: _____
PASSWORD: _____
EMAIL LINKED: _____
NOTES: _____

WHAT'S MY LOGIN ?
PASSWORD TRACKER

Website :

USERNAME: _____
PASSWORD: _____
EMAIL LINKED: _____
NOTES: _____

Website :

USERNAME: _____
PASSWORD: _____
EMAIL LINKED: _____
NOTES: _____

Website :

USERNAME: _____
PASSWORD: _____
EMAIL LINKED: _____
NOTES: _____

Website :

USERNAME: _____
PASSWORD: _____
EMAIL LINKED: _____
NOTES: _____

WHAT'S MY LOGIN ?
PASSWORD TRACKER

Website :

USERNAME: _____

PASSWORD: _____

EMAIL LINKED: _____

NOTES: _____

Website :

USERNAME: _____

PASSWORD: _____

EMAIL LINKED: _____

NOTES: _____

Website :

USERNAME: _____

PASSWORD: _____

EMAIL LINKED: _____

NOTES: _____

Website :

USERNAME: _____

PASSWORD: _____

EMAIL LINKED: _____

NOTES: _____

WHAT'S MY LOGIN ?
PASSWORD TRACKER

Website :

USERNAME: _____
PASSWORD: _____
EMAIL LINKED: _____
NOTES: _____

Website :

USERNAME: _____
PASSWORD: _____
EMAIL LINKED: _____
NOTES: _____

Website :

USERNAME: _____
PASSWORD: _____
EMAIL LINKED: _____
NOTES: _____

Website :

USERNAME: _____
PASSWORD: _____
EMAIL LINKED: _____
NOTES: _____

WHAT'S MY LOGIN ?
PASSWORD TRACKER

Website :

USERNAME: _____
PASSWORD: _____
EMAIL LINKED: _____
NOTES: _____

Website :

USERNAME: _____
PASSWORD: _____
EMAIL LINKED: _____
NOTES: _____

Website :

USERNAME: _____
PASSWORD: _____
EMAIL LINKED: _____
NOTES: _____

Website :

USERNAME: _____
PASSWORD: _____
EMAIL LINKED: _____
NOTES: _____

WHAT'S MY LOGIN ?
PASSWORD TRACKER

Website :

USERNAME: _____
PASSWORD: _____
EMAIL LINKED: _____
NOTES: _____

Website :

USERNAME: _____
PASSWORD: _____
EMAIL LINKED: _____
NOTES: _____

Website :

USERNAME: _____
PASSWORD: _____
EMAIL LINKED: _____
NOTES: _____

Website :

USERNAME: _____
PASSWORD: _____
EMAIL LINKED: _____
NOTES: _____

WHAT'S MY LOGIN ?
PASSWORD TRACKER

Website :

USERNAME: _____

PASSWORD: _____

EMAIL LINKED: _____

NOTES: _____

Website :

USERNAME: _____

PASSWORD: _____

EMAIL LINKED: _____

NOTES: _____

Website :

USERNAME: _____

PASSWORD: _____

EMAIL LINKED: _____

NOTES: _____

Website :

USERNAME: _____

PASSWORD: _____

EMAIL LINKED: _____

NOTES: _____

WHAT'S MY LOGIN ?
PASSWORD TRACKER

Website :

USERNAME: _____
PASSWORD: _____
EMAIL LINKED: _____
NOTES: _____

Website :

USERNAME: _____
PASSWORD: _____
EMAIL LINKED: _____
NOTES: _____

Website :

USERNAME: _____
PASSWORD: _____
EMAIL LINKED: _____
NOTES: _____

Website :

USERNAME: _____
PASSWORD: _____
EMAIL LINKED: _____
NOTES: _____

WHAT'S MY LOGIN ?
PASSWORD TRACKER

Website : _____

USERNAME: _____
PASSWORD: _____
EMAIL LINKED: _____
NOTES: _____

Website : _____

USERNAME: _____
PASSWORD: _____
EMAIL LINKED: _____
NOTES: _____

Website : _____

USERNAME: _____
PASSWORD: _____
EMAIL LINKED: _____
NOTES: _____

Website : _____

USERNAME: _____
PASSWORD: _____
EMAIL LINKED: _____
NOTES: _____

WHAT'S MY LOGIN ?
PASSWORD TRACKER

Website :

USERNAME: _____
PASSWORD: _____
EMAIL LINKED: _____
NOTES: _____

Website :

USERNAME: _____
PASSWORD: _____
EMAIL LINKED: _____
NOTES: _____

Website :

USERNAME: _____
PASSWORD: _____
EMAIL LINKED: _____
NOTES: _____

Website :

USERNAME: _____
PASSWORD: _____
EMAIL LINKED: _____
NOTES: _____

WHAT'S MY LOGIN ?
PASSWORD TRACKER

Website :

USERNAME:

PASSWORD:

EMAIL LINKED:

NOTES:

Website :

USERNAME:

PASSWORD:

EMAIL LINKED:

NOTES:

Website :

USERNAME:

PASSWORD:

EMAIL LINKED:

NOTES:

Website :

USERNAME:

PASSWORD:

EMAIL LINKED:

NOTES:

WHAT'S MY LOGIN ?
PASSWORD TRACKER

Website : _____

USERNAME: _____
PASSWORD: _____
EMAIL LINKED: _____
NOTES: _____

Website : _____

USERNAME: _____
PASSWORD: _____
EMAIL LINKED: _____
NOTES: _____

Website : _____

USERNAME: _____
PASSWORD: _____
EMAIL LINKED: _____
NOTES: _____

Website : _____

USERNAME: _____
PASSWORD: _____
EMAIL LINKED: _____
NOTES: _____

WHAT'S MY LOGIN ?
PASSWORD TRACKER

Website :

USERNAME: _____

PASSWORD: _____

EMAIL LINKED: _____

NOTES: _____

Website :

USERNAME: _____

PASSWORD: _____

EMAIL LINKED: _____

NOTES: _____

Website :

USERNAME: _____

PASSWORD: _____

EMAIL LINKED: _____

NOTES: _____

Website :

USERNAME: _____

PASSWORD: _____

EMAIL LINKED: _____

NOTES: _____

WHAT'S MY LOGIN ?
PASSWORD TRACKER

Website :

USERNAME: _____
PASSWORD: _____
EMAIL LINKED: _____
NOTES: _____

Website :

USERNAME: _____
PASSWORD: _____
EMAIL LINKED: _____
NOTES: _____

Website :

USERNAME: _____
PASSWORD: _____
EMAIL LINKED: _____
NOTES: _____

Website :

USERNAME: _____
PASSWORD: _____
EMAIL LINKED: _____
NOTES: _____